HOE BITCH WOMAN QUEEN GODDESS

The values of titles

By:

I. Muhammad

Copyright © 2021 by I. Muhammad

All rights reserved. No part of this book may be reproduced

or used in any manner without the prior written permission of the copyright owner,

except for the use of brief quotations in a book review.

To request permissions, contact the publisher at growordiestriving@gmail.com.

First paperback edition October 2021

Cover art by Alas Creative

ISBN 979-8-9850755-0-2 (paperback)

ISBN 979-8-9850755-1-9 (ebook)

TABLE OF CONTENTS

Intro iv
Hoe 1
Bitch 11
Woman 19
Queen 23
Goddess 37
Outro 49
About Author 51

INTRO

Ꚙ

I wrote this in hopes of redirecting why and how we visualize and treat women. For decades we've had many issues with our generations of people. The value of titles manifests how we perceive the woman. What are the values of titles? Value means the regard that something is held to deserve the importance, worth, or usefulness of something—a person's principles or standards of behavior, one's judgment of what is essential in life. Consider someone or something to be important or beneficial, have a high opinion of appreciation. Titles mean the name of a book composition or other artistic work. A word that describes someone's position or job or gives a name to this indicates the status of someone or something to garner attention and entice people to pursue and appreciate.

Many men have abused women due to not treating them as they should be treated. On the other hand, many women don't carry themselves as they wish to be treated as well. Have you noticed that women have standards and requirements for the male counterpart to be accepted to be her partner? I need a man with a house, car, money, a true King. Or I need a real man to treat me like a Queen and Goddess. The question is, does she carry herself like one? The way she carries herself will manifest whether she's even qualified or required. Many relationships don't flourish because of the disconnect, leaving them questioning where they went wrong and why they didn't survive in a relationship. Disconnection is not the only issue, but all relationships, on all levels as far as community and family. All of us, men and women, failed to know the definitions of these titles. Well, in most cases, we know the meanings but fail to live up to these titles. This is vital to our individual as well as collective growth in life. I believe that this is a part of a generational curse for our people in its entirety. And quite frankly, it is time to break these chains of ignorance and regain our true values of Kings and Queens, but for now, we're going to focus on the values of titles when it comes to women. This book is dedicated to all the women that were abused, stripped, dragged, and broken mentally, spiritually, and physically and who have lost their lives in the process. To all the mothers, sisters, grandmothers, aunties, cousins, and daughters of our people, it is time to regain the value for the black woman.

HOE

ꕥ

Hoe: A tool with a thin flat blade set across the end of a long handle used for weeding, loosening soil, etc., slang for whore, slut, or a prostitute.

Prostitute: One who engages in promiscuous sexual activity for pay. To sell oneself or talent etc., for base purposes basis, a dirty, slovenly woman. A sexually promiscuous woman, a derogatory term. What we call hoes today are all these definitions combined. The only difference is that some do it for money, drugs, or just to get satisfied. One who's had sex with a whole lot of people but repeatedly, like a parasite sucking the blood hopping from host to host.

I. MUHAMMAD

Just like that parasite, they contract whatever that host bears within their blood. When they are having sex with nearly everyone, they catch and spread diseases, STD's that is, and energy (Which is another build in itself). Even if done safely with condoms, it still is not ladylike, and over time you knock the value down, which those of our times believe. Before moving on, note that no one wants someone that everybody else has had, both male and female. It's simple, but many get it misconstrued.

Let's take a flight back to the past and the history of women, real women back then. It was frowned upon and considered ungodly or unrighteous for them to lose their virginity before marriage, both males and females really, to uphold tradition and religious beliefs and remain pure. In some cultures, the man can have more than one wife, and in some, just one wife, meaning polygamous or monogamous. Polygamous meaning more than one, while monogamist means only one. A woman in those times who went against those beliefs was considered either a mischief-maker or, some say, homewrecker or worse, the works of the devil. She was bashed as the no-good, foul, disrespectful, negative unpurified being to roam the land, man to man.

Committing adultery in some cultures was punishable by death but also frowned upon greatly. These days and times we live in now are totally different. People manipulate religious morals and principles to fit their physical, dire desires. They are no longer waiting until marriage to be deflowered by the one who is deemed worthy. Youngsters are also losing their virginity just as young as 11 or 12 years old, becoming sexually active. Most of them were not taught properly to ensure safety and maintain purity, dignity, respect, and honor to mature into grown women. Therefore, most get pregnant at an early age and go downhill from there. They can't finish school because they are pregnant and have to find a job. Most girls don't have support from family, so they sign up for government aid to kick in, and guess what? They still do what they have been doing and, by that time, have gotten worse, imitating what they see on TV and music videos. Who do we blame?

Ourselves!

Nowadays, we believe that it is OK to have many sex partners if we are single and practice safe sex. Or as long as we are on a polygamous basis where all counterparts agree to

I. MUHAMMAD

whatever terms agreed upon by the collective. For us men, we don't see it as bad as women; of course, we're speaking about monogamy. But there's really no difference. We say it all the time, "man, I want a lady in the streets and a freak in the bed." Meaning a woman that knows how to carry herself in public who's mature and lives by true principles and morals as a grown, dignified woman. And when it's time to get freaky, she can satisfy her man sexually; however that may be. Done vice versa holds no honor, dignity, nor respect. Follow me, the definition for hoe is basically a gardening tool; what's being cultivated? What kind of seeds are being sowed and planted? What kind of flowers are being nurtured? Maybe the beautiful flowers that bloomed are being destroyed by the tool, or are they the tool?

From the TV shows to the songs on the radio, to the albums of our favorite artist, to the streets we walk upon, it shows us that a hoe is one who has sex with everybody and anybody. Remember, these are traits of a prostitute, which is a sex tool like the garden tool hoe is used for gardening. Being used, abused, and dragged through the mud to only be forgotten once the job is done. You could find her on the corners or anywhere unclean within drug-infested areas. We all know all hoes are not drug addicts or can be found in drug-infested areas but also some of the most common areas, which is anywhere. She's used for her services and moves on to the next. Once again, not all hoes are prostitutes; some are just overly and uncontrollably sexually active and can't control their lower desires. Some women are emotionally damaged to the point where they distrust any man for fear of being hurt, which is unbearable. On the flip side, most are insecure, always thinking their lover is cheating. Also, some women are emotionally damaged and suffer from traumas from when they were young. Their traumas were caused by other men who had molested or raped them to the point where they acted in such a fashion. That results in the women not wanting to get attached nor catch feelings, just meet, have sex, and bounce. Drama and mixed emotions due to hardship and pain from most no good, dishonorable men, who take them and their tender love for granted—not noticing that they leave themselves open to a whole lot more like pregnancy, sexually transmitted diseases, etc.

How many women have said we were just having fun, but I don't want to be tied with him forever, let alone to have him be the father of my child. I'm not ready! Giving birth to

I. MUHAMMAD

a heap of unwanted problems, baby mama drama as we know it in the hood. He ain't nothing; I can't stand him; I hate him! Why set themselves up? For fun or sexual satisfaction with no strings attached here, is it worth it? Why gamble? Some are even getting abortions, and then the talking starts. Not saying you should worry about what people say; but people say presentation is everything. What man wants a woman that has three different baby fathers and that has three or four abortions? That sounds, to most men, to just hit and get out of there rocky! You got too much going on! It's sad, but most men think like this. Sound familiar? This is where the cycle comes from with our youngsters.

Quick retract to sum it up. Children follow us because we are their role models and follow these same footsteps, get pregnant, drop out, don't graduate, and can't go to college because the father is too young and doesn't know true responsibility. He, in return, drops out also, being sucked in the whirlwind of the streets. Subjecting him to the ills of the street life because he can't find a job, or the job doesn't pay enough, so he either desires to rob people or sell drugs. We all know the ending result of that, either the graveyard or prison. The child grows up without a father and a mother with no education until she tightens up and gets her education to handle business. Still, all the weight is on her shoulders now, simply by following our footsteps in ways and actions when they are morally wrong. See the ripple effect?

Think of this, the same hoe tool can be rented but instead of this hoe being rented for a fee. This hoe is stolen, then brought back after used and rundown for the next person to do the same thing. For example, I once knew a girl who was super sexy, and I mean top-notch. Well, I hollered at her and got her number, and not only did I feel good, I thought, *yes, I pulled a bad one! Boy, she's bad; wait till the boys see her they going to hate!* It was already instilled in my mind; I'm just going to hit a couple of times then on to the next. She called, and we hooked up, and the feeling I initially had was killed dramatically. The sex was nothing like I thought, and her body was nothing like what was broadcasted, and I felt like there was no challenge at all. *It was way too easy*, I thought to myself. Afterward, she spread like an epidemic, sad to say. Next thing you know, even the dudes who were considered not cool had her. She was considered the hood or project hoe. Nobody wanted to have sex with her anymore because she was having sex with everyone. Back then, we had an ill way of thinking, I do admit. But eventually, she had a couple of STD's which I thank God I didn't receive; and a whole lot of kids; thank God I didn't conceive. There's that ripple effect again.

Analyze yourself and observe your actions. Are they like this girl or a prostitute? If you carry yourself and have the identity of a hoe, which is a tool, then that's how you will be treated. What's the value of a hoe? $5, $10, $100, etc.? Whatever it is will never amount to the actual value of a woman, which is priceless. To regain dignity and respect from such a reputation, simply stop having sex with everybody and anybody, stop allowing yourself to be so available to everybody. Like Steve Harvey said, "stop giving the cookie to every open jar in the kitchen for trade, sexual satisfaction, or fear of commitment."

No man, no real man wants a woman that's too easy, and that's been with everybody. Real kings yearn for real queens! You have to struggle for the things you need and want in life. Almost like a game, nobody, and I mean nobody, wants to play a game that has levels that are too easy to be won or conquered. Yeah, we all want to have fun, but the fun begins after the objectives in the mission for love are met. Each level gets harder and more complex, and only true warriors are victorious at the end of the game. I firmly believe that the best things in life we must struggle, fight, and bleed for. You will appreciate it more. And it's OK to be sexy, but some things are best to be left a mystery until requirements are met from the counterpart. Make him respect your mind first then he will respect your body and soul. The body without the mind and soul is just an empty vessel, a hollow shell. Cover yourself with the royalty of 1000 Queens that you were born with and gifted by God since the beginning of time. I challenge you when you meet the next guy; make him wait and see how long he remains. That time in-between will not only let you know if he's in it for the long run. Still, it will show you if both are compatible with laying down the foundation to build a nation. If you are still stuck on that 'I do what I want, can't nobody tell me nothing' type thing, just notice the guys high fiving, celebrating, laughing, and comparing sex stories of you with each other. Now how does that make you feel? I once thought like that until my eyes were opened to reality.

BITCH
ॐ

Bitch; Female dog. A bitch is a female dog; female dogs are raised, trained, chained, and utilized for breeding to gain currency and pride. Or a female animal companion that answers your every beckoned call, only knowing or trained to obey and follow directives for self-gratification. Why consider yourself an animal? Sexually men love a woman who can tap into her animal instincts for a stronger sexual drive in the bedroom and increase sexual satisfaction. But there are limits like the saying goes, 'lady in the streets but a freak in a bed.' The word bitch is now considered a title for ratchet females. Ratchet meaning a classless way of calling someone brash and ignorant, also known as off the chain, wild, out of control. Basically, like either a ride-or-die female in the drug game or simply a female with an HBIC attitude like a female dog. This title bitch was adopted like the word from our oppressors, aka slave masters, to identify black women as bitches and black men as niggers. Neither should have been adopted as such in the first place. It is morally wrong, so wrong. Take it back to history in the 80s, real righteous women such as honorable Queen Latifah in the song when she says, "Who you calling a bitch?" She corrected this title and label that she didn't want to be labeled by because she is a woman, a queen, a goddess. Like other queens such as Aretha Franklin, established such a thing as in the song 'RESPECT' due to not only being disrespected countlessly by white men but also by black men and the rest of the world just for being born a melanated woman. The list goes on and on because these and other real righteous black queens strived as much as possible to correct such an ill label and title. There are many labels and titles that we used or use nowadays and adopted from animals, such as 'kid' from goats, to describe her children and offspring. Dog from dogs to define who your right-hand man was pertaining to homies or homeboys. We can go on and on, that's another subject. We should know what animal's characteristics to learn from and adapt just for their pure natural will to survive. As we use lions, gorillas, eagles, and bears, etc. Something that an old-school elder said a long time ago always stuck with me. He quoted, "A man can never do anything to a woman unless a woman allows him to do so in any other cases other than by brute force." So basically, we men for generations called women bitches and have been doing it for so long that most women now accept it and label themselves as such. A perfect example is the Rick Ross song I used to listen to "I need a real bitch 365 let her count the cheese, let her see the pies." He and so many other rappers glorify such a thing, and the listeners promote and accept it. Then on the flip side, the great king 2Pac had a song called "And you wonder why we call you bitch". To me, that was a powerful song with a powerful message, basically saying we call you bitch because that's how you carry yourself. You accept such an ill title when you're so much more. Another song that I admired from 2Pac, "Keep your head up," gave a powerful message for black women of all shapes and sizes. Like when he stated, "I wonder why we take from our women, why we rape our women. I think it's time to kill for our women, time to heal our women, be real to our women," and I so agree! But the worst thing of all is that we are teaching our seeds and raising them to carry on such ill titles and labels, thinking it's cute. Not taking the time to correct ourselves to teach them and raise them properly on morals, principles, respect, honor and dignity. And the same song 'keep your head up' explains this the best in the verse "why must we create a race of babies, that will hate the ladies, that make the babies. Since a man can't create one, he has no right to tell a woman where and when to make one, so will the real men get up". That's real. But it's not all on us men to correct; it's on the women as well, the ones that are comfortable with calling themselves bitches. Let's compare this to the 'you are what you eat' saying. The label you have is how you will be treated, so if you, as a woman, label yourself and carry the title of a bitch; a female dog, you would most definitely be treated like a dog, so why get mad when you embrace it? And men treat you as such and dog you out? Then you have the nerve to say all men are dogs or worthless! You attract what you display. So, when you stop labeling yourselves as bitches, female dogs, stop and correct the man that does also and stop carrying yourself as such. Then this cycle will change; if not, you will always have a value of a true bitch. Does anything else really need to be explained any further? Every day it appalls me when I constantly hear young women accepting and promoting such negativity. Think about times in the days of our ancestors.

They never referred to our women as bitches but more like queens. Probably would have been killed for such a display of ignorance and disrespect. May I quote the same song from 2Pac "you wonder why we call you bitch?" How can we be taken seriously by others by such a broad display of ignorance as a collective? Then wonder why we have so many laughing, mocking, and disrespecting us every chance they get because we disrespect ourselves. The hip-hop industry is part of this problem by exploiting, glorifying, and selling such garbage. When hip-hop was birthed, we were still striving to pull together as a people to unify as a collective, consolidated force. Hip-hop was a gateway to spread righteous and real messages to the people through songs like 'Fight the power' from Public Enemy. 'Self Destruction' by a vast majority of famous, well recognized, and respected MCs of that era that decided to band together on one track to send the most powerful message, *Self*

I. MUHAMMAD

Destruction. As the generations changed, so did the definition of real respect, love, loyalty, honor, and morals in the same projects and hoods of black America. I have been subjected to this as we all have, but my mother never taught me to identify a woman by the title of a bitch. Instead, she showed me the difference and showed me how to honor and respect all women no matter how they carry themselves. At the same time showed me what kind of woman a king is supposed to be compatible with in order to correct and build a foundation on love. To build a kingdom and give birth to many nations with a queen, a real queen. She and life taught me that whatever title or label you give yourself is what you live up to. Like our government name studies show, whatever names were given to us at birth, we tend to live by the characteristics defined by them. So once again, if you consider yourself a bitch and allow others to identify you by it, then guess what? You will be treated like one when you are so much more than that title and label, bitch, a female dog. Start now and regain your respect, dignity, and honor by first respecting and honoring yourself in a dignified manner. Remember, you can buy a dog, but you can never buy a woman because her worth is priceless. Enough said, right?

WOMAN
ೋ

An adult female human being. I stumbled upon something during my research that states, "Being a woman means having a strong sense of identity, accepting your body as one that adapts and changes over time, being confident and building up the people in your life." It means you have the wisdom to be grateful for what you have while still being hungry enough for growth. Proverbs 31 says, "She is clothed with strength and dignity; she can laugh at the days to come, she speaks with wisdom and faithful instruction is on her tongue. She watches over the affairs of her household. She does not eat the bread of idleness, a valuable member of society, strong-willed". In my opinion, a woman is not only a fully developed woman physically but, overall, the maturity of the mind. This woman stands on morals and principles while enduring her cycles of nature, still finding balance for her kingdom in the sense of energy.

As I've pointed out before, the woman can and is the original teacher of the children they bear. Upon birth, it's in our nature to cling to the mother for further development and survival. Feeding and keeping us warm with her physical body. What about the women who don't bear children, you ask? Are they any lesser than the woman who bears a child? My answer is no to a degree; I believe just the fact of knowing you can bear a child based on gender is enough. It's the genetic nature of every woman regardless; women have power that we constantly try to understand. For the most part, we have collected many studies and theories of womankind, but some things are still a mystery. In a nutshell, women are expected to be "superhuman," which I believe is a fact! But a lot of people don't consider that it's a struggle to be a woman. Society has placed the burden of struggles on women since the beginning of time, which has evolved dramatically in our times, especially the black woman. The feminine energy can change the whole sea of masculine energy upon the grace of her presence. A real woman stands firm on love, integrity, dignity, honor, and respect.

She does this for herself first. By carrying herself in such a manner manifests a demand for respect and honor from humanity. The great Queen Maya Angelou wrote, "Pretty women wonder where my secret lies, I'm not cute or built to suit a fashion model's size, but when I start to tell them, they think I'm telling lies. I say it's in the reach of my arms, span of my hips, The stride of my step, The curl of my lips; I'm a woman phenomenally, phenomenally woman, that's me. I walk into a room just as cool as you please, and to a man, the fellows stand or fall down on their knees. Then they swarm around me, its hive of honeybees. I say it's the fire in my eyes, and the flash of my teeth, The swing in my waist, and the joy in my feet. I'm a woman phenomenally, phenomenally woman, that's me. Men themselves have wondered what they see in me. They try so much, but they can't touch my inner mystery; when I try to show them, they say they still can't see. I say it's in the arch of my back, the sun of my smile—The ride of my breast, the grace of my style. I'm a woman phenomenally, phenomenally woman, that's me.

I. MUHAMMAD

Now you understand just why my heads not bowed. I don't shout or jump about or have to talk really loudly. When you see me passing, it ought to make you proud. I say it's in the click of my heels, the bend of my hair, the palm of my hand, the need of my care, cause I'm a woman phenomenally, phenomenally woman, that's me."

I could break down what the Great Queen Mother Goddess Maya Angelou scribed, but we'll just let her words season the plot. A real woman is matured not only physically but mentally. She's comfortable in her skin and knows what she wants and needs in her life. She strives tirelessly each day to conquer past and current daily struggles that life brings upon her journey—at the same time, striving to reach and accomplish her goals. Note: we're building on what a real black woman is, not just women collectively.

QUEEN
ଔ

The female ruler of an independent state, especially one who inherits the position by right of birth. The most powerful chess piece that each player has, able to move any number of obstructed squares in any direction along a rank, file, or diagonal on which it stands— a reproductive female in a colony of social ants, bees, wasps, etc. A Queen is a woman who doesn't bow or conform to what others think of her but takes advisement from others because she knows that she doesn't know it all. A Queen, a woman who rules a country or kingdom. Who is highly respected and valued by other people. She fights for the rights of the people of the kingdom under her rulership. She's compassionate because she understands the hardships and struggles of life due to the experiences she's endured personally and collectively. She is humble because she does not exploit the people by abusing her position of authority for selfish purposes.

Now let's break it down further as to the Queen in the home. You may ask, what nation or kingdom does she rule? Her kingdom is herself as well as her home. I say this because her body is her temple in which her mind and spirit embodies. In the house, she rules her nation of loved ones, whoever they may be—nurturing nursing and teaching them from the aspects of the feminine energy or role. As far as her body, she carries herself with royalty by constantly valuing her qualities of self. Her victories of conquered struggles manifest her respect by nature. Reigning supreme by defeating the odds produced by society's status quo. She's well fitted for the crown due to the wisdom gained by her daily struggles. Here I will give a few examples of true black Queens.

The first example will have to be my mother, as I identify as Queen of Queens, or some may even say Queen Mother. In my home, she was the first example of what a real woman, Queen, and Goddess was and how they should be treated and valued. I've seen my mother struggle many times growing up, not truly understanding the entirety of what was going on and how it would affect us. Her being a true queen, she never let the struggles of society's ills captivate her growth, responsibilities, and obligations. We didn't have water or lights at times, doing what she had to do for her kingdom. Times she sacrificed eating just because there wasn't enough food, so she did so to ensure we were fed and full. Being a single mother with the absence of help in the projects or hood, she did her absolute best. She taught us generational wealth by always creating jobs for herself and showing us each step of the way. She was constantly building with us intellectually and making us read to keep us sharp mentally and spiritually. She carried herself with such elegance and magnitude of respect. She was humble but didn't take any disrespect. She took care of her physical by eating healthy and her mind by consistently learning and applying the wisdom gained. She took care of her soul by submitting to her belief in Islam to the will of God to reach her highest self. I can write a subatomic scribe that stretches ions just by explaining the example my mother was to us. I will say that because of her, we know the difference and know the actual value of women. For that, her kingdom will birth other kingdoms that, as a collective, breathes life to a whole nation of people.

Other examples will be Queen Amintu, daughter of Bakwa Turunku, who was a great Hausa warrior. She is well known as a warrior princess, having inherited her mother's assertive and precise nature. Her mother built the capital of Zazzau. The city was one of the seven original states of Hausaland in the 16th century. As a member of the royal family, Amina chose to hand her military skills. She soon became one of the greatest warriors of Zazzau. She increased Zazzau's borders through her intelligent tactics. Her leadership helped to make Hausaland the center of trade in the Saharan and West African region. She was also the architect of Hausaland's fortified walls. Her career as a warrior princess spanned over three decades.

Queen Nefertiti was a prominent Queen from ancient Egypt, meaning "a beautiful woman has come." Leaving a legacy of beauty, strength, and power. She married Akhenaten, who ruled Egypt from 1353 to 1336 BC—

bearing six children, including King Tut (Tutankhamun). Together they were known for their exploits in expanding the Egyptian nation. Responsible for establishing the cult of Aten. The religion placed the sun god Aten as an essential figure of worship. She's known as a woman of authority and power!

Queen Makeda, Queen of Sheba, Ethiopia's 14th-century royal epic, the Kebra Nagast or "Galaxy of Kings," wrote that Makeda was a Queen of incredible strength. She survived a battle with the Serpent King Awre. The Serpent King was troubling the Northern Ethiopian Kingdom of Axum. After defeating the Serpent King, Makeda rose to power as the Queen of Axum. She's also known for her relationship with King Solomon of Jerusalem. They had a son named Menelik or (Ebna La- Hakim or Ibn Al-Hakim), meaning "Son of the Wise." Their son became the first imperial ruler of Ethiopia and the first of a line of Aksumite Kings. Makeda and her son brought back the biblical ark of the covenant to Axum; through them, the lineage of Great East African and Nubian Kings were born. Leaving the legacy as an important figure in the Old Testament history for the Ethiopian Orthodox Church.

I. MUHAMMAD

Queen Ranavalona, the first of Madagascar, ruling from 1788 – 1861. She was of Merina descent, which is the island's largest ethnic group. Reigning for 33 years, she created Madagascar to be an independent state. She remained defiant against the powers of European colonialism. Therefore, maintaining the cultural and political sovereignty of her nation. The colonialists viewed her as a tyrant, while her people saw her as a patriotic leader. – Before I continue, I want you to reflect on these great examples of Queens in history. As we read, these Queens weren't just Queens; they were warriors who fought for the rights of the people and what they believed in—also rewriting cultural history for their people and kingdom that affects our present. They define the Black Queen as a highly respected and resilient woman of African descent in our modern time. These women are highly respected for how they carried themselves and how they had self-respect. While being resilient in the hardships of being a woman of power, which many feared, or just being a regular woman. Now here are some Black Queens of our time.

Queen Angela Davis who's an educator and activist known for her involvement in a politically charged murder case in the early 1970s. Influenced by her segregated upbringing in Birmingham, Alabama, Davis joined the Black Panthers and an all-black branch of the communist party as a young woman. She also became a professor at UCLA but fell out of favor with the administration due to her ties, of course. She was then charged with aiding the botched attempt of imprisoned Black Radical George Jackson, serving an 18-month term in jail before she was acquitted in 1972. She has since then returned to teaching as a professor and authored several books. As a teenager, she organized interracial study groups, which were constantly interrupted by the police.

Queen Assata Shakur is considered a leading figurehead in the 70s Black Liberation Army. She was charged with murder and sentenced to life in prison in 1977—ultimately escaping and making it to the FBI's most-wanted list to this day. As it states in the early hours of May 2, 1973, Assata Shakur was stopped on the turnpike by a state trooper named James Harper, allegedly for driving with a faulty rear light. In the car with Shakur were fellow Black Liberation Army members Zayd Malik Shakur and Sundiata Acoli. In a second patrol car was trooper Warner Foerster. Minutes after they pulled over, both Zayd Malik Shakur and Trooper Foerster were dead, and Assata and Trooper Harper were shot and wounded. In 1977, Shakur was convicted on one murder charge and six assault charges and sentenced to life in prison. Escaping in 1979 with the assistance of BLA members posing as visitors and has been a fugitive since. She's now listed as the top 10 most wanted terrorists. Assata Shakur was simply another target for the FBI and COINTELPRO because she was a strong black woman, a part of the BLA. She's also Tupac Shakur's aunt. Taught by her grandparents, who always told her, "I want that head held up high, and I don't want you taking no mess from anybody. Don't you let me hear anybody walking over my grandbaby." That was the start of her legacy, empowering the black community and other Black Queens to join and fight the cause.

Queen Rosa Parks helped initiate the Civil Rights movement in the United States when she refused to give up her seat to a white man on an Alabama bus in 1955. Her actions inspired the leaders of the local black community to organize the Montgomery bus boycott. The boycott was led by a young Rev. Dr. Martin Luther King Jr; the boycott lasted more than a year. It was recorded that she lost her job at that time—only ending when the United States supreme court ruled that bus segregation was unconstitutional. Later she became a nationally recognized symbol of dignity and strength in the struggle to end entrenched racial segregation.

Once again, I'd like for you to pause and reflect on their struggles as black women in the times of Civil Rights and Jim Crow. Reflect on how their ways and actions affected not only them but the nations of our people then and now. Notice anything that was repeated or that they all have in common? Reflect on actually being in these settings of time, from ancient empires to racism where our people had their own sections of dwellings not by choice but by disrespectful force for the only fact of being colored. Where we were lynched, cut, shot, hung, hosed with fire hoses as we ran and jumped from the devil's hounds known as K9s. Overall, it was tough being an African American man or woman. Have your thoughts become heavier sinking in the black hole of the pondered? Can you feel it? Can you hear it? Can you smell it? Can you see it? If the answer is yes, then say it aloud! YES! If the answer is no, I advise you to reflect deeper, regardless of whether yes or no; I urge you to continue reading. These examples of Queens are acknowledged as being the backbone of the Civil Rights movement.

Queen Ella Baker is acknowledged as the most influential woman in the movement as the founder and strategist. She started her journey in the National Association for the Advancement of Colored People (NAACP) in 1940 as a field secretary and later director of branches. In 1957, Ella Baker helped Martin Luther King Jr. organize the Southern Christian Leadership Conference in Atlanta, Georgia, and ran a voter registration program. After the Greensboro, NC sit-ins, she left the SCLC to assist new emerging student leaders at Shaw University in April 1960.

Queen Diane Nash was one of the Civil Rights movements, significant organizers. A co-founder of the SNCC and helped orchestrate the Nashville, Tennessee campaign to integrate lunch counters. In 1960 Nash attended the founding meeting of the SNCC in Raleigh, North Carolina, and in 1961 she supported the ten students in Rock Hill, South Carolina. They were arrested in protest activities and refused bail. Nash and three other activists were also jailed in Rock Hill in 1961. Nash was a leader in the

Mississippi Freedom Rides, which was the Congress of Racial Equality (CORE) project. She served as the liaison between the press and the US Department of Justice from her Nashville base. In the summer of 1961, she became the head of SNCC direct action campaigns.

Queen Mary McLeod Bethune, the daughter of former slaves and one of 17 children, was an American educator, Civil Rights activist, stateswoman, humanitarian, and philanthropist. She aimed to improve educational opportunities for African Americans and is best known for starting a school in Daytona Beach, Florida, that later became the Bethune Cookman University. She also served as president of the National Association of Colored Women in 1924 and in 1935 became one of the founders of the National Council of Negro Women. She was a friend of Eleanor Roosevelt and became the highest-ranking African American woman in government. President Franklin Delano Roosevelt named her director of Negro Affairs of the National Youth Administration in 1936.

Queen Dorothy Height was called the godmother of the Civil Rights movement because of her all-embracing involvement in the fight for Civil Rights that began in the 1930s. Height met McLeod Bethune at a New York YMCA and became her right-hand woman joining the national staff in 1944. Height helped organize events for the movement, including the march on Washington for MLK. She was a strong advocate for women's rights and served as the National Council of Negro Women president. She and other black women leaders held a parallel march of women down Independence Avenue while the men marched down Pennsylvania. Her affiliation with the NCNW continued into the 1990s.

Queen Ruby Bridges became a pioneer when she was at the age of six. She was the first African American child to integrate into a public school in Louisiana. She had to be escorted to William Frantz Elementary in New Orleans by her mother and three US Marshals because of threats of violence. Only one teacher was willing to teach her, and she was the only black child in her class. She could not eat lunch in the cafeteria or participate in recess because of threats, but this brave child, beyond her years, never missed a day of school.

Next will have to be Coretta Scott King, who I feel was a leader in her own right by the continuation of her late husband's endeavors. She experienced discrimination and segregation at Antioch College in Ohio, where she studied music; Coretta joined the NAACP, helping to raise awareness and funds for the cause both nationally and internationally. She married Martin Luther King Jr in 1953; after his death, she continued to fight for civil rights. She founded the MLK Jr Centers for Nonviolent Social Change to continue his legacy.

I stopped the full details of each Queen because I figured the point was clear. Now that I've defined what a Queen was and gave examples from ancient to modern times. All these Queens have many things in common, which are respect, bravery, and dignity. They stood their ground, crown up, and fought physically, vocally, mentally, and spiritually. And due to their efforts of strength and resilience, it marked the beginning of a new age for our people and women as a whole. Eventually, whether ancient or modern-day, we all are affected by these queens' footprints in history. They fought, loved, and conquered, gaining the respect of their reigns of power forever through time, making them queen

I. MUHAMMAD

legends that time will never allow to be forgotten. The question is to the women reading this, can you relate in some way to these examples? Do you have the love to carry on the legacy of your king as Coretta Scott King did? Do you fight the battles of the struggle placed by society like these warrior queens who fought through sweat, guts, and tears? Are you highly respected based upon the individuality of your character and conduct? Do you have the character and conduct of one? To the men reading this, can you identify these characteristics in the women in and out of your life? If you can identify, do you truly respect them as such? These questions I ask for you all to reflect upon before moving on to the next chapter.

GODDESS

೧೩

Goddess, a female deity. A woman who is adored, especially for her beauty. A female being who is believed to control the world or part of it or represents a certain quality. Any sort of God, deity, or anything that is worshiped that is of the female origin. A beautifully brilliant and wholesome woman, she is simply not like any other woman on earth. Therefore, she possesses an uncommon spiritual element that cannot be solely defined that is clearly present. Beautiful, intelligent, magical, and perfect. She was often worshipped by ancient religions such as the Greeks, Romans, and Egyptians. Goddesses are also prominent in pagan religions. A Goddess has many qualities like peacefulness, purity, representing women as a whole, and other "God-like" attributes. I've personally heard plenty of tales of what a Goddess was, and one stuck out the most. I read one day that the black woman or Goddess was the highest form of God. In my spiritual journey, I was enlightened that all of humanity should reach their higher selves, which is the God or goddess level of self. Here we're honing in on the Goddess only, of course. For a woman to grow, develop, and mature, she must go through these stages of life until she reaches her fullest potential, which is her highest self. Let me stop there before we continue! The higher self can be associated with many belief systems describing an eternal, omnipotent, conscious, and intelligent being. To be eternal means to be infinite, everlasting, endless, but by its nature without beginning or end in time, existing at all times, always true and valid. Omnipotent meaning almighty, having virtually unlimited authority or influence/God. Conscious, meaning perceiving or noticing facts or feelings Personally felt (self-guilt) capable of or marked by thought, will, design, perception, self-conscious, mentally alert or active, awake; done or acting with critical awareness "to know." Are you keeping up? If you've answered yes, good! If not, just follow me, but either way, I desire you to continue reading!

My definition of a Black Goddess is a woman who has awakened the inner-G. Her inner essence of Godly degrees of her physical, mental, and spiritual being. By gaining true insight of her benevolent form manifesting her truest nature mirroring the universe and mother nature. She bares the balance of creation and destruction, peace, and chaos. She possesses the power of energy and its shifts but while using it wisely in a righteous manner. In our generation, she's not blinded by materialism, nor is she a slave to technology. She's the true architect of civilization. I once read that the woman is classified as the mother of civilization. Men carry the life cell, but the woman bares and births the nation. She is creating the growth and development process in triple darkness, also known as the womb, which also mirrors the black matter of the universe. She is the first teacher of civilization, showing us the degrees of love. Now let's travel to the examples of Goddesses in ancient times.

Goddess Ma'at, an ancient Egyptian deity said to be core to the conceptions of the universe's rules and in maintaining balance and divine order. Ma'at represents pure truth, balance, order, and justice. Projecting order and harmony being the daughter of Ra, the Sun God, and wife of Thoth, the God of wisdom. Ma'at goddess of divine and cosmic order, truth, justice, and balance. She's represented as a woman who wore a crown with a single ostrich feather in her headdress, also known as the winged Goddess. The totem was a stone platform that defined the stable foundation on which order was constructed; the primeval mount is also said to first originate from the waters of Nun or Chaos. The ancient Egyptians believed that after a person dies, their soul is taken into the "Hall of double justice" by the God of wisdom Thoth. In the presence of other gods like the Lord of the dead, Osiris. Along with 42 assessors of judges of Ma'at accompanying her.

Here the heart believed to be the essence of a person is weighed in the scales of justice with the feather from Ma'at's headdress or crown on the other side. There would be balanced scales for those with a good life, but for those who have committed injustice, the heart would weigh heavier. After, the soul of the person would be eaten by the Goddess Ammut. The balanced hearts will be led to Osiris by Ma'at, where they were granted to join the celestial gods for eternity. Ma'at ruled over all three worlds; even the other gods had to obey her rulings.

Goddess Isis, the Goddess of protection, motherhood, and magic. Isis, an Egyptian Goddess of Ancient Egypt, name meaning (the seat) Eset, which refers to her stability and throne of Egypt. She was viewed as the mother of every pharaoh through the king's association with Horus, Isis's son. Also known as the Queen of the throne, her crown was the empty throne of her murdered husband, Osiris. Her symbols are the scorpion that kept her safe when she was hiding, a kite, the falcon shape she assumed in bringing her husband back to life, the empty throne, and the sistrum. Isis is portrayed as the selfless, giving mother, wife, and protectress who places others interests and well-being ahead of her own. Let's not forget Isis is known as "Weret-Kekau" (the great magic) for her power and "Mut-Netjer" (the mother of the Gods). Still, it's recorded that she has many attributes.

Goddess Amesimi, a Kushite protective Goddess and wife of Apedemak (The Lion God), is represented with a crown resembling a falcon or a crescent moon on her head, top of which a falcon was standing. In the north front reliefs of the Lion Temple in Naqa, she appears together with Isis, Mut, Hathor, and Satet. Compared to the Goddesses of ancient Egyptian origin, Amesemi seems to be much more, which is typical for the representation of the women of Meroe. Amesemi is a Nubian Goddess carrying a divine essence everywhere she goes and possesses divine beauty. She was described as having dark brown skin, full lips, with dark-colored eyes. Enchanting all with her divine beauty making no difference, men or women all fell under the thrall of the Goddess. In her time, she styled her hair into what resembled a crown or chalice, also with loose curls. There are way too many Goddesses recorded in history to bring to the forefront. Goddesses such as in Yoruban belief Egungun-Oya, Iyami-Aje, Oba, Oshun and Yemoja. Or in Zulu tradition, Mamblambo (The Goddess of Rivers), Mbaba-Mwana-Waresa. But with all that you've read, all these Goddesses were unique in their own ruling of authority and purpose as well as the representation of women on many, many levels. Here we will hone in on their qualities, characteristics, personalities, as well as nature only. All women possess these divine qualities; it's just a matter of being aware and striving to tap in and activate the growth of these qualities and characteristics. Also known as the essence of God in Self, which is pure power. The Supreme Goddess with love, life, loyalty, knowledge, wisdom, understanding, balance, order, selflessness, justice, strength, resilience, peace, respect, harmony, bliss, science, mathematics, as above so below, as within as without. She is the alchemist; she is the magical process of transformation, creation, or combination. Taking something ordinary and turning it into something extraordinary, sometimes in ways that can't be explained. She's achieved the impossible; she is a leader, teacher, divine sacred mother, universal unifier, sacred keeper of wisdom, and healer. For one of the last examples, allow me to introduce you to Audley Moore, better known as the "Queen Mother," a Harlem Civil Rights Activist. She was born July 27, 1898, in New Iberia, Louisiana. After her parents passed away, she dropped out of school to be a hairdresser to provide for her two younger sisters. She educated herself from the scribes of Frederick Douglas and listening to the speeches of Marcus Garvey. Her heart was pricked by the sharpened words of the Black Nationalist message from

Marcus Garvey's speech in New Orleans. She then made the pilgrimage to Harlem, New York. The year was 1922, which was the blooming year of the Harlem Renaissance. Then becoming a member then leader in Marcus Garvey's Universal Negro Movement Association known as the UNIA. After the demise of the UNIA, she created several other organizations. She served as the founder and president of the Universal Association of Ethiopian Women in the year 1950. Later in 1963, she birthed the Committee for reparations for the descendants of United States Slaves. The Republic of New Africa, which in fact demanded self-determination, land, and reparations. The Queen Mother presented a petition to the United Nations at the height of the Cold War in 1957. This petition's requests of land and billions of dollars in reparations for the descendants of African slaves on top of the direct support for African Americans who requested to immigrate to Africa. In 1972 she attended the funeral of the former President Kwame Nkrumah to show her respect. Where in fact, the Ashanti group granted her the honorary title "Queen Mother." She last attended the Million Man March in 1995, then passed away May 2, 1997, at the age of 98 years old of natural causes.

You may be wondering why I chose to use the Queen Mother as the last example. Queen Mother means a woman who is a dowager Queen, the mother of the reigning monarch. The term has been used at the least since 1560 in England. It arises in heredity monarchies in Europe and is also used to describe a few similar yet distinct monarchical concepts in non-European cultures worldwide. A monarch is the head of state for life or until abdication, and therefore the head of state of monarchy. A monarch may exercise the highest authority in the state, or others may wield that power on behalf of the monarch. Usually, a monarch either personally inherits the lawful right to exercise the state's sovereign rights or is selected by an established process from a family or cohort eligible to provide the nation's monarch. By the Queen Mother Moore educating herself thus introducing her endeavors to aid and assist in our nation's struggle in which her service, thoughts, concepts, ideas, etc., crowned her of such royalty.

I. MUHAMMAD

Now that we have the history, I can then continue to explain why she's mentioned. In my humble opinion, she eventually tapped into her highest self or Goddess within. By educating herself on the knowledge of self as well as elevating her awareness to truly see and know and understand deeper what the struggle was and what she could do to sprout solutions to these problems of our nation of people. That's a Goddess because her deeds will live on through the generations to come. She showed love, respect, honor, order, justice, which we most definitely needed as a people, along with many other traits and qualities of a true black Nubian Goddess. Let's take a moment to reflect upon each Goddess that was mentioned in this chapter. They may have had different duties or purposes of their eras, but they all share the same qualities and attributes in some form or fashion. All women have these powers deep within them upon birth; it's just a matter of the elevation of the woman. I believe that we as a people, both men, and women as a collective whole, have an obligation to enlighten these young queens upon birth that they possess such powers as a Goddess. We just have to rid our minds of the ill mindsets we developed from the sufferings from the powers that be. Now I'll pose a question, now that we've defined what a Goddess is as well as plenty of historical examples. The question to the women is, are you vibrating in your higher self? Do you possess pure divine love, life, loyalty, knowledge, wisdom, understanding, innerstanding, over-standing, respect, balance, selflessness, honor, true omnipotence, the beauty within, as well as utilize and apply for the greater good of self as well as the collective? To the men, do you acknowledge the actual value of these Goddesses when you're in the presence of one? Do you protect their integrity and dignity? Do you assist her with your undying aid for her to reach this level of being just by doing your part as a God? These are questions you should ask yourself and ponder upon but on a global scale!

OUTRO

ॐ

We have discussed and built upon what a Hoe, Bitch, Woman, Queen, and Goddess is. Note, our people have developed the ability to take negative words or gestures used to disrespect us and switch the narrative for empowerment. Like the word bitch, where we see black women as well as others utilizing the word in a resilient form of energy. Yes, there are many degrees of these titles, but the focal point is knowing that our women are so much more. They are astronomical beings that walk the face of the earth and rule upon the universe. May my divine words of wisdom and understanding prick your hearts, minds, and spirits. I would like to thank all the women I've met in life as well as those I've personally learned from or built with for this project to be manifested into a reality. I've learned to appreciate women more due to my personal experiences with women I've hurt and loved. By learning more about myself as far as the good, the bad, the beautiful and ugly of self in order to grow and develop into a better version of self, who realized he's a God in his own right. With that being said, I want to dedicate this to all the women who were devalued due to ignorance, self-hatred, discrimination, race, and the negatives that society has laid at our feet. And to all the women who have paved the way for us through sweat, guts, blood, and tears for the betterment of nations. Thank you and infinite gratitude to you all, and with that, I leave as I came…

Lastly, what would you rather be respected and identified by of the Hoe, Bitch, Woman, Queen, and Goddess?

ABOUT AUTHOR

ɔɕ

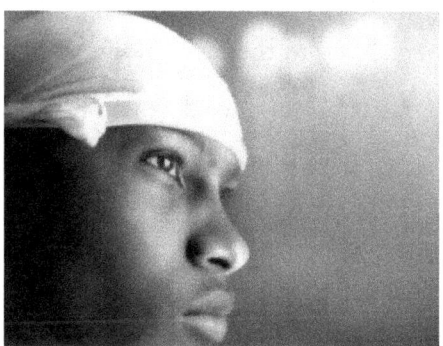

I. Muhammad, originally from Staten Island, New York, migrating south to Pensacola, Florida, with his mother and two older siblings for better opportunities. Born and raised in a Muslim household was strict in ways, but that was out of protection from the ills of society and what was going on just a few feet away from their doorstep. His mother, Brooklyn raised, nationalities of Sudanese,

I. MUHAMMAD

Cuban and Indian, who was also community-based. She was always willing to uplift the people—seeking various careers such as singing at the Apollo before the great migration to the south. His father was absent, which is where he gets his Trinidadian roots. Growing up in the projects or hood was the best of both worlds, in the home filled with intellectual conversations, surahs, prayers but also hardships. Being raised by a single Sunni Muslim mother of then four, three boys, and one girl before the last boy making five, later in life, upon migration from Florida to South Carolina. He watched the chaos from the windows having to lay on the floor when shots rang out. To peek back up to the sites of crime scene tape—watching the bright lights from police cars, crime scene lamps, blue and red lights from police cars and ambulances, as well as helicopters. Whether it was from the windows of the houses or fire escapes from the buildings he lived in or anywhere he laid his head called home. Being the middle child of five was hard. Still, he always received unconditional love from his mother while also putting her through the most during the struggles of school. Eventually leading him to that world that he watched from those windows, porches, and front yards, diving deep in the middle of it all—the best of both worlds. Which eventually led to 30 years of incarceration for voluntary manslaughter. Now in the pen, looking out a smaller blocked window seeing the world from the inside out. No matter the struggles or choices he made, his mother taught him morals and respect for women and their values no matter their shade, size, and race. But also observing what she went through as a single parent until the day she got married. He saw how she was treated by a great man who respected and treated her like a woman, Queen, and Goddess.

www.ingramcontent.com/pod-product-compliance
Lightning Source LLC
Chambersburg PA
CBHW071415290426
44108CB00014B/1840